german
shorthaired
pointer

understanding and
caring for your breed

Written by
Sue Parr

german shorthaired pointer

understanding and
caring for your breed

Written by
Sue Parr

Magnet & Steel Ltd

Unit 6 Vale Business Park, Llandow, Vale of Glamorgan,
United Kingdom CF71 7PF

Printed and bound in China through Printworks Global.

ISBN: 978-1-906305-81-9
ISBN: 1-906305-81-1

Acknowledgements

The publishers would like to thank the following for help with
photography: Tracy Morgan (www.animalphotographer.co.uk), Sue and
Alan Parr (Pruso), Maureen Nixon, Eileen Hughes (Sonnenberg) and
John Staite (Brucourt).

Contents

Introducing the German Shorthaired Pointer

The German Shorthaired Pointer is the ultimate all-rounder. He was bred to perform multiple roles in the hunting field, and although he is still highly valued as a gundog he has evolved to become the most versatile of pet dogs. He is a loyal and loving companion and also has the talent to be a star performer in a range of canine sports.

The German Shorthaired Pointer is a WYSIWYG dog – what you see is what you get, and this is true in terms of both physical appearance and temperament.

He is a medium-sized dog, strong, athletic and muscular, with a short coat that hides nothing. He has clean lines, a glossy coat and striking markings. His finely-chiseled head is framed by floppy ears, and his large, dark, melting eyes show great intelligence and good humour. He has a distinctive aristocratic bearing, which gives him an air of superiority.

Breed characteristics

The German Shorthair was bred as a hunting dog, but his role as a family pet is of equal importance. He is an intelligent, bold, and characteristically affectionate dog that is co-operative and easily trained.

The GSP loves interaction with humans and is an ideal pet for an active family that will provide an outlet for his energy. Most German Shorthaired Pointers make excellent watchdogs as they are alert to all comings and goings.

When he is among friends, a GSP will greet visitors with boundless enthusiasm, either jumping up or wagging madly from his nose to the tip of his tail. He will usually have a gift in his mouth, which will be the nearest object he can find, whether it be a toy, a shoe, or a cushion, and he may talk to you as well. He may squeal or rumble, or he may bark excitedly – whatever he does, you will definitely be made to feel welcome!

Like all dogs, German Shorthaired Pointers are pack animals and whether he lives with other dogs or just a human pack he needs to know his place, otherwise he will quickly try and promote himself to pack leader. The old saying: 'give him and inch and he will take a mile' sums up the GSP's attitude to life, and your German Shorthair will run circles around you if you don't establish leadership early on.

Trainability

The Breed Standard, the written blueprint for the breed, calls for the German Shorthaired Pointer to be biddable. In theory, that means training him is easy; he will do anything because he wants to please you!

German Shorthaired Pointers are capable of learning a great deal and from a very young age. From four to six weeks the GSP starts to learn and this does not stop until the day he passes on. We had an old lady of 15 who in the last months of her life learnt how to open and raid the fridge.

This is a dog with an independent mind, and although he has good focus when he is working, he is easily distracted by exciting sights, sounds, and scents. Some German Shorthairs can be wilful and obstinate, and some are a little manipulative. It is important to be 100 per cent consistent in training so your dog respects you and understands where the boundaries lie.

Lifestyle choices

The German Shorthaired Pointer is eager to please and will adapt to differing circumstances. However, there are a few essentials to bear in mind.

This is a high-energy breed that needs plenty of exercise and activity. This need for exercise (preferably off lead) coupled with the breed's natural instinct to hunt, means that training is an absolute necessity, and that can't be stressed enough.

Failure by the owner to give this active and intelligent dog sufficient exercise and proper training can produce a German Shorthaired Pointer that appears to be hyperactive, or has destructive tendencies. Bored GSPs are famous for chewing through stud walls, skirting boards and furniture and ripping the stuffing out of cushions and sofas. Therefore, this breed is not a suitable pet for an inactive home or for inexperienced dog owners.

The German Shorthaired Pointer is usually very good with children and seems to be attracted to them. Perhaps he sees them as equal pack members because they are no threat to him, or because they share the same energy levels.

This is a sociable breed that gets along with other dogs, but care should be exercised with small animals that are kept as pets, such as cats, rabbits and guinea pigs; poultry can also be a temptation. The GSP has a strong hunting instinct, and this needs to be tempered in a domestic setting. A well-mannered GSP should, if handled and trained properly, live in harmony with other animals.

Life expectancy

We are fortunate that the German Shorthaired Pointer is generally a very healthy breed, and, with luck, he should survive into his early teens. The average life expectancy is 12 to 14 years.

Tracing back
in time

As his name implies the German Shorthaired Pointer hails from Germany, where hunters wanted to breed a robust dog that found, flushed and retrieved game tenderly to hand.

The GSP is a breed of dog that has been established in continental Europe for generations, with more or less the same conformation. They come from the same ancestors as all the other pointing dogs to be found in Europe, collectively known as hunt, point, retrievers (HPRs).

These versatile sporting dogs were bred to carry out all the tasks required in the hunting field rather than using specialists: Pointers and Setters to locate game, Spaniels to flush it out and Retrievers to bring the game to hand.

The all-round hunt, point, retrieve breeds, were developed in a number of European countries and include the Weimeraner and the Large Munsterlander, also from Germany, the Hungarian Vizsla, plus the Italian Spinone and the Bracco Italiano.

In the mix

The first authentic reference to a pointing dog comes as far back as the 13th century. An Italian, Brunetto Latini, was exiled in France in 1260 and wrote:

"Others are brachs with falling ears, which know of beasts and birds by their scent; therefore they are useful for the hunting."

It is thought that there are several different breeds behind the GSP so he could be classed as a bit of a mongrel. The Spanish Pointer, described by some as a big, coarse and somewhat clumsy dog was probably crossed with the lighter English Pointer. There is also mention of Bloodhound, Foxhound and a St Hubert Hound in the GSP's make up.

The breed became established during the 19th century, bearing a strong resemblance to the dogs we recognise today. They were predominantly liver dogs – some with a flash mix of white hairs, others with an even mixture of liver and white hairs giving a salt and pepper effect to the coat, now known as ticking.

The aim was to produce a dog with a nose that could hunt and find game, with good tracking sense and the stamina to follow the scent of wounded game, tenacious enough to work in dense cover and in water, and brave enough to take on the larger animals that were found in the forests of Germany.

The three breeds

As the German Shorthaired Pointer was being developed, two other breeds of German Pointer were also being created. The German Wirehaired Pointer, bred from Griffon, Pudelpointer, Deutscher Stichelhaar and Deutscher Kuzhaar, and the German Longhaired Pointer, which resulted from crossing Setters, Pointers and Spaniels.

The three Pointers have obvious differences in coat type as well distinctive features in conformation and temperament which means they are recognised as three separate breeds. The German Shorthaired Pointer is the most popular of the three, but the Wirehair and Longhair both have a dedicated following.

Developing the breed

The German Shorthaired Pointer was highly valued as a hunting dog in his native home, and it was not long before news of this handsome, talented breed spread overseas.

America was ahead of the game in establishing the German Shorthaired Pointer outside Germany. It is thought that the US discovered the breed as far back as the 1880s, when many immigrants came to the US from Europe, bringing their dogs, or news of their home-bred hunting dogs, with them.

The first clear documented evidence was that of an avid hunter called Dr. Charles Thornton. In 1925 he imported a bitch of Austrian/German descent called Senta von Hohenbruch. This was followed shortly afterwards by several other German-bred dogs acquired by keen hunters in Minnesota, Nebraska and Wisconsin.

Following this influx of GSPs, the American Kennel Club (AKC) officially recognised the German Shorthaired Pointer in 1930, and the breed has gone from strength to strength.

Coming to Britain

At the turn of the last century, a handful of German Shorthaired Pointers were bought over to compete at Crufts, but the breed failed to catch on. It was not until the 1940s, shortly after the end of World War Two, that GSPs started to arrive in the UK in numbers.

The breed was recognised by the Kennel Club and awarded Challenge Certificates in 1955 and Field Trial status in 1963. With good support both in the show ring and the field, the GSP arguably became the most successful dual purpose gundog in the Gundog Group, with nine dual title holders – Champions in field trials and in the show ring – in its brief history in this country.

Sadly, we may have seen the last of the dual Champions in the UK, although there is not a split of type in the breed as such. There are a few kennels that compete in shows and trials, but it seems that none of the owners of the big showing kennels compete in field trials, and the die-hard field trialling fraternity do not compete in the show ring.

However, the German Shorthaired Pointer continues to make his mark in both disciplines, with entries growing ever larger at Championship shows.

What should a GSP look like?

The aristocratic German Shorthaired Pointer draws admiring glances wherever he goes with his beautifully proportioned body that is designed for power, endurance and speed. So what makes a GSP so special?

If you speak to most German Shorthaired Pointer owners they will tell you they have the perfect GSP and, of course, they do. Pet owners are not looking for perfection as in the world of show dogs; they are looking for the dog that is perfect for what they want. As long as he is obedient, has a good temperament and is easy to live with, he is perfect in their eyes.

In the world of show dogs, the perfect dog does not and will never exist; every dog has his faults. All breeders can do is strive to produce a dog that is fit for function and adheres as closely as possible to the Breed Standard, which is the written blueprint

describing what the breed should look like. In the show ring, the judge does not compare dog against dog, but each dog against the Breed Standard. The dog that, in their opinion, comes nearest to the Standard, is the winner. However the Breed Standard is open to interpretation and because of this you don't get the same dog winning all the time.

Across the world there are three main Breed Standards for the GSP. The original Breed Standard is from the Federation Cynologique Intenationale (FCI) which is the governing body for 86 countries, including Germany – the breed's homeland. The Kennel Club (KC) in the UK and the American Kennel Club (AKC) have drawn up their own Standards, which show some differences in detail.

General appearance

The German Shorthaired Pointer is typified by his noble bearing and well-proportioned body that denotes superb athleticism. He has graceful clean-cut lines and a proud attitude. The American Standard states that a dog in "hard and lean field condition" should not be penalised. This emphasises the point that the GSP is, first and foremost, a working breed.

Points of anatomy

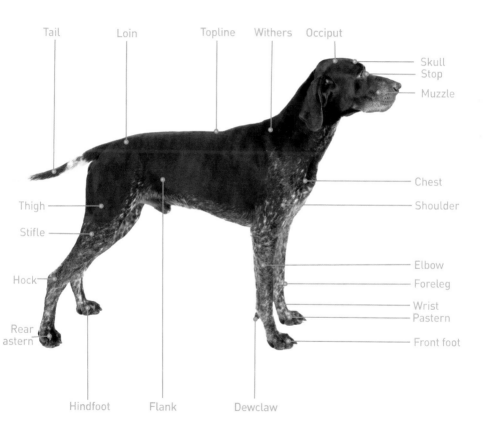

Tail

Loin

Topline

Withers

Occiput

Skull

Stop

Muzzle

Chest

Shoulder

Thigh

Stifle

Elbow

Foreleg

Hock

Wrist

Pastern

Rear
pastern

Front foot

Hindfoot

Flank

Dewclaw

Temperament

The GSP's temperament is everything you could ask for – steady, reliable, biddable, gentle and affectionate. He is very loyal and shows keenness for any type of work. He is extremely versatile, working on land and in water, and will show great perseverance when he is using his nose.

Head and skull

The best description of the GSP's head is "clean-cut"; it should not appear too light nor too heavy, and should be in balance with the body. Male and female characteristics should be instantly recognisable.

The skull is reasonably broad, arched on the sides and rounded at the top. The foreface rises gradually from the nose to the forehead, and there is no definite stop (the step up between the muzzle and the forehead) which would be typical of a Pointer. However, when viewed from the side, there is an appearance of a stop because of the eyebrow.

The muzzle must be sufficiently long to allow a working dog to carry game; the length should equal the length of the skull. The nose protrudes slightly and should have wide, mobile nostrils. It should be brown in colour, except in black and black roan dogs, which have a black nose. The FCI Standard states that dogs that have white as their basic colour may have a flesh-coloured or spotted nose, but the American Standard is more severe, stipulating that a spotted nose is not desirable and a flesh coloured nose is a disqualifying fault.

Eyes

The eyes are medium-sized and almond-shaped, neither protruding nor too deep-set. The ideal colour is dark brown, although the UK Standard allows for the shade to vary depending on coat colour. Light eyes are considered highly undesirable.

The expression which comes from the eyes is all-important; it is described by the American Standard as "full of intelligence and expression, good-humored and yet radiating energy".

Ears

The German Shorthaired Pointer has broad ears that are set high – just above eye level – and lie close to the head. When laid in front the ear extends to the corner of the mouth. The ears should not be too fleshy, nor too thin, and should be rounded at the tip.

Mouth

This is a dog that is designed to retrieve game and so strong jaws are essential. The lips are well developed but should not overhang, and the teeth should meet in a perfect scissor bite with the teeth on the upper jaw closely overlapping the teeth on the lower jaw.

Neck

The length of the neck should be in harmony with the general appearance of the dog, progressively thickening towards the body. It should be muscular and slightly arched and the skin should not be loose fitting.

Forequarters

The shoulders are sloping, very muscular, and the shoulder blades lie flat. The elbows are well laid back, neither pointing outwards nor inwards, and the forelegs are straight, lean, muscular and strong. The pasterns (equivalent to the bones in our hands and feet) are slightly sloping.

Body

The German Shorthaired Pointer is a short-backed breed but should still stand over plenty of ground. The chest is deep rather than wide, but, most importantly, it should be in proportion to the rest of the body. The ribs are deep and well sprung, and the back is firm. The loin (the dog's 'waist') is wide and slightly arched.

Hindquarters

The rear assembly provides the power, so the thighs must be strong and well muscled. The stifles (the dog's 'knees') are well bent, and the hocks (the dog's 'ankles') are square with the body and slightly bent. It is the angulation of the stifle and hock joints that produce the necessary drive and traction.

Feet

The feet are compact and close knit; they are round or 'spoon' shaped. They should be well padded and the toes should be well arched with strong nails. In common with many of the gundog breeds that retrieve from water, the GSP's feet are webbed.

Tail

Customarily, the German Shorthaired Pointer had a tail that was docked to half its natural length, and this is still permissible in the USA and for working dogs. However, show dogs in countries governed by the FCI and by the Kennel Club in the UK will have a full, natural tail which reaches to the hocks and is carried horizontally or just below the line of the back.

Gait/movement

A German Shorthaired Pointer in full flow is a
sight to behold – his harmonious, balanced strides
emphasise his nobility. His gait is smooth and lithe,
and as he moves from walk to a faster speed, the
legs converge beneath the body, which is known as
'single-tracking'. The front legs reach well ahead,
effortlessly covering the ground, and the hind legs
provide forceful propulsion.

Coat

The coat is short and flat, and is coarse to the touch.
It is slightly longer on the underside of the tail, and
is softer and thinner on the ears.

Colour

This is a somewhat controversial issue as far as
the three Breed Standards are concerned. The
UK Standard is very precise, stating there are two
colours – liver and black – and these may be solid or
with a combination of white which includes patched,
ticked or roan markings.

The American Standard makes no mention of black
GSPs and is very definite on any exceptions to the
accepted liver colour. However, black GSPs can be
registered and therefore compete in field trials, but
they cannot be shown.

The FCI Standard is basically the same as the UK, but it states yellow tan markings are permissible.

The colour of the liver varies from a light almost chocolate colour to liver that looks almost black. All these variations are correct.

Size

The American and UK Standards give a size guide of males 58 to 64cm (23 to 25in) at withers and females 53 to 59cm (21 to 23in). The FCI ask for dogs to be 62 to 66cm and bitches 58 to 63cm, allowing for a slightly bigger dog at the bottom end of the scale. However, the majority of judges agree that the most important consideration is that a dog should appear well balanced.

Summing up

Although the majority of German Shorthaired Pointers are kept as pet dogs or working dogs and will never be exhibited in the show ring, it is important that breeders strive for perfection and try to produce dogs that adhere as closely as possible to the Breed Standard. This is the best way of ensuring that the GSP remains sound in mind and body, and retains the characteristics that are unique to this very special breed.

What do you want from your GSP?

There are hundreds of dog breeds to choose from, so how can you be sure that the German Shorthaired Pointer is the right breed for you? Before you take the plunge into GSP ownership, you need to be 100 per cent confident that this is the breed that is best suited to your lifestyle.

Companion

The German Shorthaired Pointer is loving, loyal and biddable. He is quick to learn and eager to please and, in common with many of the gundog breeds, he has made the transition from working dog to companion dog with ease.

This is a wonderful breed if you have children, as the GSP likes nothing more than to join in with family activities. He can be a little exuberant in his youth, so care should be taken if you have small children, but with training and supervision, he will learn to curb his enthusiasm.

The German Shorthair will also enjoy life with slightly older owners; he will thrive on being the centre of attention, and as long as his owners are fit and active and enjoy walking, he will want for nothing.

This is not the ideal breed for the very elderly, as the German Shorthaired Pointer is too demanding in terms of exercise. He is medium-sized, but he is surprisingly strong – particularly true of male GSPs – so he is not a good choice for those who are a little frail or unsteady on their feet.

In terms of general care, the German Shorthair is a no-nonsense breed and his short coat is easy to care for.

Gundog

If you want to train a dog to the gun, or compete in Field Trials, you need look no further. The German Shorthaired Pointer is the perfect all-rounder, relishing the tasks of hunting, pointing and retrieving. He is highly intelligent and loves to work.

He is possibly a little more sensitive than some of the other gundog breeds, such as the Labrador Retriever, and this appeals to many sporting owners.

If you are serious about working your German Shorthaired Pointer in the field, you would be advised to find a breeder that has a record of producing successful gundogs.

Show dog

Do you have ambitions to exhibit your German Shorthaired Pointer in the show ring? Many of the gundog breeds have become divided into show types and working types, and look very different from each other. However, this is not the case with the GSP and, theoretically, a top-class working dog should meet all the criteria of the Breed Standard and be able to win prizes in the show ring.

Having said this, if your plan to focus on showing your German Shorthair, you need to find a breeder that specialises in producing show quality stock. You then need to assess a litter to find a puppy with show potential, then train him so he will perform in the show ring, and accept the detailed 'hands on' examination that he will be subjected to when he is being judged.

It is also important to bear in mind that not every puppy with show potential develops into a top-quality specimen, and so you must be prepared to love your German Shorthair and give him a home for life, even if he doesn't make the grade.

Sports dog

The German Shorthaired Pointer is a talented all-rounder and he is a brilliant choice if you want to get involved in one of the canine sports. He has a strong work ethic and will be only too happy if you ask him to use his brain. He will adapt to the precision required in Obedience, make use of his natural athleticism in Agility and Flyball, and employ his excellent sense of smell when it is needed for tracking.

For more information, see Opportunities for GSPs page 154.

What does your GSP want from you?

A dog cannot speak for himself, so we need to view the world from a canine perspective and work out what a German Shorthaired Pointer needs in order to live a happy, contented and fulfilling life.

Time and commitment

First of all, a German Shorthaired Pointer needs a commitment that you will care for him for the duration of his life – guiding him through his puppyhood, enjoying his adulthood, and being there for him in his later years. If all potential owners were prepared to make this pledge, there would be scarcely any dogs in rescue.

The German Shorthair is a 'people dog'; he was bred to work closely with his handler in the field, and sees his owner as the centre of his universe. He will not be happy if he is expected to spend lengthy periods on his own without human interaction. He will become bored, and this may lead to destructive behaviour or excessive barking.

If you cannot give your GSP the time and commitment he deserves, you would be strongly advised to delay owning a dog until your circumstances change.

Practical matters

The German Shorthaired Pointer is a smart-looking dog, and he achieves this with the minimum of care from his owner. His short, waterproof coat needs no more than a weekly brush, which is perfect for owners with limited time. However, all dogs need to be checked on a regular basis to ensure that any signs of health problems are spotted at an early stage.

In terms of exercise, a German Shorthaired Pointer needs the opportunity to use his body – walking, running, and investigating scents. If you are an active, outdoors person, exercising your GSP will be one of the great pleasures of dog ownership, even if this does mean going out in all weathers!

Mental stimulation

Catering for your German Shorthaired Pointer's physical needs is essential, but providing sufficient mental stimulation must also come high on your list of priorities.

The GSP is a clever dog, bred to work. If his brain is under-occupied, he may well adopt his own agenda and develop anti-social behaviour, which will make him difficult to live with. It is your job to educate him, and to channel his mental energy.

Initially, you need to work on training and socialisation, which are key ingredients in creating a dog that is content with his role in the family and is able to cope with the stresses of modern life. Then you need to give your German Shorthair a role in life so that he feels fulfilled. This could mean working your dog in the field, or getting involved in one of the canine sports. But if this is not for you, you can do some fun training – playing retrieve games, hide-and-seek, or teaching him some party tricks. It doesn't matter what you do as long as you are spending quality time with your GSP and giving him the mental stimulation that he needs.

Extra considerations

Now you have decided that a German Shorthaired Pointer is the dog of your dreams, you can narrow your choice so you know exactly what you are looking for.

Male or female?

The choice between male or female boils down to personal preference. Males can be just as placid and loving as females and likewise, an assertive female can be just as much of a problem as an assertive male. Generally speaking there is not a lot of difference in the temperament of either sex, it really depends on how they are bred and how you bring them up and train them. So don't be put off if you set your heart on a bitch from a particular litter and there are none available; don't discount a sound well-bred male puppy.

If you opt for a female, you will need to cope with her seasons, which will start at around seven to eight months

of age and occur approximately every nine months thereafter. During the three-week period of a season, you will need to keep your bitch away from entire males (males that have not been neutered) to eliminate the risk of an unwanted pregnancy.

Many pet owners opt for neutering, which puts an end to the seasons, and also and has many attendant health benefits. The operation, known as spaying, is usually carried out at some point after the first season. The best plan is to seek advice from your vet.

An entire male may not cause many problems, although some do have a stronger tendency to mark, which could include the house. However, training will usually put a stop to this. An entire male will also be on the lookout for bitches in season, and this may lead to difficulties, depending on your circumstances.

Neutering (castrating) a male is a relatively simple operation, and there are associated health benefits. Again, you should seek advice from your vet.

Colour

There is some degree of choice when it comes to colour preference. There are two colours: liver (which should not be referred to as brown or chocolate) or black. A GSP can be solid liver, liver and white, liver and ticked or liver, white and ticked with the same variations in black, but they should never be tri-coloured. Large patches of liver across the back of the dog are sometime referred to as saddles.

Generally the head and ears of the GSP are a solid colour, but sometimes there may be a blaze down the foreface. A non-solid coloured puppy is born with bright white patches and, as the dog matures, the white patches start to colour in; this is called ticking. There is no right or wrong pattern to the markings – anything goes. However from a showing point of view, an odd line of marking may give the appearance of structural imbalance.

Liver and liver and white German Shorthairs are easier to come by, but the gene pool of black and black and white dogs has expanded in recent times with imports from Europe

German Shorthairs are basically black or liver, with or without white markings.

More than one?

German Shorthaired Pointers can become addictive, and before you know where you are you will want more. There is also the temptation to have two puppies together, to keep each other company. In my opinion, in inexperienced hands, this is a disaster waiting to happen.

A responsible breeder would never sell you two puppies from the same litter, and if this was suggested, I would walk away and go somewhere else because the breeder is obviously struggling to sell their pups.

Looking after one puppy is hard work, but taking on two pups at the same time is more than double the workload. House training is a nightmare as, often, you don't even know which puppy is making mistakes, and training is impossible unless you separate the two puppies and give them one-on-one attention. It is a win-win scenario for the puppies; they will never be bored as they have each other to play with. However, the likelihood is that they will form a close bond with each other, and you will come a poor second.

If you do want a second GSP, wait until the first one is about two years old. By this stage his training will be well underway, he will have established his place

in the family and you will have more experience of the breed.

Occasionally, you may have squabbles amongst dogs in the same household. This is generally triggered by a dispute, usually over food or a toy, but it's over in a matter of seconds with no damage done. In some breeds you hear of dogs falling out, and it reaches a situation where they can never be together again. Fortunately, this rarely happens with German Shorthairs. They are very sociable dogs; in the shooting environment you will often have several dogs traveling together in the back of the game cart between drives, and there is no hint of trouble.

An older dog

You may decide to take on an older dog instead. Such a dog may be harder to track down, but sometimes a breeder may have a youngster that is not suitable for showing, but is perfect for a family pet. In some cases, a breeder may re-home a female when her breeding career is at an end so she will enjoy the benefits of getting more individual attention.

There are advantages to taking on an older dog, as you know exactly what you are getting. But the upheaval of changing homes can be quite upsetting, so you will need to have plenty of patience during the settling in period.

Re-homing a rescued dog

We are fortunate that the number of German Shorthaired Pointers that end up in rescue is still relatively small.

In many cases, a GSP ends up in rescue through no fault of his own. The reasons are various, ranging from illness or death of the original owner to family breakdown, changing jobs, or even the arrival of a new baby. However, there are GSPs that are put up for rescue because their owners have failed to give them the exercise and mental stimulation that is essential for the breed and, as a result, behavioural problems have developed.

It is unlikely that you will find a German Shorthair in an all-breed rescue centre, but the specialist breed clubs run rescue schemes, and this will be your best option if you decide to go down this route.

Try to find out as much as you can about a dog's history so you know exactly what you are taking on. You need to be realistic about what you are capable of achieving so you can be sure you can give the dog in question a permanent home.

Again, you need to give a rescued GSP plenty of time and patience as he settles into his new home, but if all goes well, you will have the reward of knowing that you have given your dog a second chance.

Sourcing a
puppy

Your aim is to find a healthy puppy that is typical of the breed, and has been reared with the greatest possible care. Where to start?

A tried-and-trusted method of finding a puppy is to attend a dog show where your chosen breed is being exhibited. This will give you the opportunity to see lots of different German Shorthaired Pointers. When you look closely, you will not only see a variety of colours and markings, you will also be aware of different 'types' on show. They are all purebred GSPs, but breeders produce dogs with a family likeness, so you can see which type you prefer.

When judging has been completed, talk to the exhibitors and find out more about their dogs. They may not have puppies available, but some will be planning a litter, and you may decide to put your name on a waiting list.

Internet research

The Internet is an excellent resource, but when it comes to finding a puppy, use it with care:

DO go to the website of your national Kennel Club.

Both the American Kennel Club (AKC) and the

Kennel Club (KC) have excellent websites which will give you information about the German Shorthaired Pointer as a breed, and what to look for when choosing a puppy. You will also find contact details for specialist breed clubs (see below).

Both sites have lists of puppies available, and you can look out for breeders of merit (AKC) and assured breeders (KC) which indicates that a code of conduct has been adhered to.

DO find details of specialist breed clubs.

On breed club websites you will find lots of useful information which will help you to care for your GSP. There may be contact details of breeders in your area, or you may need to go through the club secretary. Some websites also have a list of breeders that have puppies available. The advantage of going through a breed club is that members will follow a code of ethics, and this will give you some guarantees regarding breeding stock and health checks.

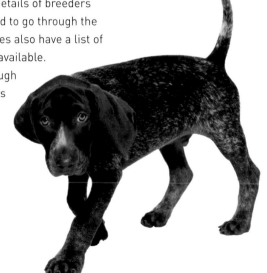

It takes an expert to evaluate show potential.

DO NOT look at puppies for sale.

There are legitimate breeders of German Shorthaired Pointers with their own websites, and they may, occasionally, advertise a litter, although in most cases reputable breeders have waiting lists for their puppies. The danger comes from unscrupulous breeders that produce puppies purely for profit, with no thought for the health of the dogs they breed from and no care given to rearing the litter. Photos of puppies are hard to resist, but never make a decision based purely on an advertisement. You need to find out who the breeder is, and have the opportunity to visit their premises and inspect the litter before making a decision.

Never buy a puppy if you can't see him with his mother and never buy from a person who says they will meet you somewhere or send the puppy to you. Good breeders will want you to meet their dogs in their own homes.

Questions, questions, questions

When you find a breeder with puppies available, you will have lots of questions to ask. These should include the following:

- Where have the puppies been reared? Hopefully, they will be in a home environment which gives them the best possible start in life.

- How many are in the litter?

- What is the split of males and females?

- What colours are available?

- How many have already been spoken for? The breeder will probably be keeping a puppy to show or for breeding, and there may be others on a waiting list.

- Can I see the mother with her puppies?

- What age are the puppies?

- When will they be ready to go to their new homes?

Bear in mind puppies need to be with their mother and siblings until they are eight weeks of age otherwise they miss out on vital learning and communication skills which will have a detrimental effect on them for the rest of their lives.

You should also be prepared to answer a number of searching questions so the breeder can check if you are suitable as a potential owner of one of their precious puppies.

You will be asked some or all of the following questions:

- What is your home set up?

- Do you have children/grandchildren?

- What are their ages?

- Is there somebody at home the majority of the time?

- What is your previous experience with dogs?

- Do you have plans to show or work your GSP?

The breeder is not being intrusive; they need to understand the type of home you will be able to provide in order to make the right match. Do not be offended by this; the breeder is doing it for both the dog's benefit and for yours.

Be very wary of a breeder who does not ask you questions. He or she may be more interested in making money out of the puppies rather than ensuring that they go to good homes. They may also have taken other short cuts which may prove disastrous, and very expensive, in terms of vet bills or plain heartache.

Health issues

In common with all purebred dogs, the German Shorthair suffers from some hereditary problems so you need to talk to the breeder about the health status of breeding stock and find out if there are any issues of concern. GSPs can be affected by hip dysplasia, so both the sire (father) and dam (mother) should have had their hips X-rayed and scored, and the relevant paperwork should be available to view (see page 187).

Puppy
watching

Viewing a litter

It is a good idea to have mental checklist of what to look out for when you visit a breeder. You want to see:

- A clean, hygienic environment.

- Puppies who are out-going and friendly, and eager to meet you.

- A sweet natured mother who is ready to show off her pups.

- Puppies that are well covered, but not pot-bellied, which could be an indication of worms.

- Bright eyes, with no sign of soreness or discharge.

- Clean ears that smell fresh.

- No discharge from the eyes or from the nose.

- Clean rear ends – matting could indicate upset tummies.

- Lively pups who are keen to play.

It is important that you see the mother with her puppies as this will give you a good idea of the temperament they are likely to inherit. It is also helpful if you can see other close relatives so you can see the type of German Shorthair the breeder produces.

In most cases, you will not be able to see the father (sire) as most breeders will travel some distance to find a stud dog that is not too close to their own bloodlines and complements their bitch. However, you should be able to see photos of him and be given the chance to examine his pedigree and showing/working record.

Companion dog

If you are looking for a GSP as a companion, you should be guided by the breeder who will have spent hours and hours puppy watching, and will know each of the pups as individuals. It is tempting to choose a puppy yourself, but the breeder will take into account your family set up and lifestyle and will help you to pick the most suitable puppy.

Working dog

If you are looking for a puppy to train as a shooting companion or to compete in field trials, you will need to go to a breeder who specializes in producing this type of GSP. A working dog should still look like a typical GSP and meet the stipulations of the Breed Standard, but you want a dog that comes from proven working lines. You will be more interested in temperament, wanting the drive, keenness and perseverance of this versatile hunting breed, rather than focusing on the more showy attributes of dogs that are exhibited in the ring.

When choosing a working puppy, look for a lively individual who is interested in everything that is going on. In addition, you want a puppy that is eager to play, shows a willingness to retrieve, and is responsive to your body language and your voice.

Show dog

If you are buying a puppy with the hope of showing him, make sure you make this clear to the breeder. A lot of planning goes into producing a litter, and although all the puppies will have been reared with equal care, there will be one or two that have show potential.

Ideally, recruit a breed expert to inspect the puppies with you, so you have the benefit of their objective evaluation. The breeder will also be there to help as they will want to ensure that only the best of their stock is exhibited in the show ring.

It is important to bear in mind that puppies go through many phases as they are developing. A promising puppy may well go through an ugly duckling phase, and all you can do is hope that he blossoms! However, if your GSP fails to make the grade in the show ring, he will still be an outstanding companion who will be a much-loved member of your family, and there is always the opportunity to compete in other disciplines with him.

Sports dog

The German Shorthaired Pointer can be trained to a high level in a number of the canine sports, including obedience, tracking, working trials and agility. A good number of these GSPs have come from working lines, but show-bred GSPs have also been highly successful as they retain the willingness to work, and the eager-to-please attitude that is so important.

If you looking for a sports dog, try the same tests as for a working dog, focusing on those who want to interact with you, and who show real enthusiasm when you produce different toys.

A GSP-friendly home

It may seem an age before your German Shorthair puppy is ready to leave the breeder and move to his new home. But you can fill the time by getting your home ready, and buying the equipment you will need. These preparations apply to a new puppy but, in reality, they are the means of creating an environment that is safe and secure for your GSP throughout his life.

In the home

Nothing is safe when a puppy is about – and the German Shorthaired Pointer is no exception. A GSP puppy will investigate everything he comes across with his mouth – and his teeth – and he can be surprisingly destructive if something takes his fancy. Not only does this mean that your prized possessions

are under threat; it could also have disastrous consequences for your puppy if he swallows indigestible objects, or gets hold of cleaners and other chemicals which could be highly toxic.

The best plan is to decide which rooms your GSP will have access to, and make these areas puppy friendly. Trailing electric cables are a major hazard and these will need to be secured out of reach. You will need to make sure all cupboards and storage units cannot be opened – or broken into. This applies particularly in the kitchen where you may store cleaning materials, and other substances, which could be harmful. There are a number of household plants that are poisonous, so these will need to relocated, along with breakable ornaments.

While your GSP is growing, his joints are vulnerable so you need to reduce the risk of injury. Most owners find it is easier to make upstairs off-limits right from the start. The best way of doing this is to use a baby gate; these can also be useful if you want to limit your GSP's freedom in any other part of the house.

In the garden

Secure fencing is essential for the German Shorthaired Pointer, who is sufficiently athletic to make a leap for freedom. Although these dogs form very strong attachments with their owners, a bored GSP that receives insufficient exercise may feel compelled to take it upon himself and find a way out.

GSPs can escape from enclosures that are 1.2 m (4ft) in height – sometimes higher – with little difficulty, so you should think in terms of providing fencing that is a minimum of 1.5m (5ft). Regular exercise and training, or other vigorous activity like agility, can alleviate this desire to escape.

If you are a keen gardener, the best plan is to protect your plants from unwanted attention by fencing them off so you have a 'people' garden and a 'dog' garden. GSPs are great diggers, and can turn a lawn into a bombsite in no time!

You will also need to designate a toileting area. This will assist the house training process, and it will also make cleaning up easier. For information on house-training (see page 94).

House rules

Before your puppy comes home, hold a family conference to decide on the house rules. You need to decide which rooms your puppy will have access to, and establish whether he is to be allowed on the furniture or not. Remember, with a German Shorthair, it is important to start as you mean to go on. You cannot invite a puppy on to the sofa for cuddles only to decide in a few months' time that this is no longer desirable. A GSP needs to know where his boundaries lie. If house rules are applied consistently, he will understand what is – and what is not – allowed, and he will learn to respect you and co-operate with you.

Buying equipment

There are some essential items of equipment you will need for your German Shorthaired Pointer. If you choose wisely, much of it will last for many years to come.

Indoor crate

Rearing a puppy is so much easier if you invest in an indoor crate. It provides a safe haven for your puppy at night, when you have to go out during the day, and at other times when you cannot supervise him.

A puppy needs a base where he feels safe and secure, and where he can rest undisturbed. An indoor crate provides the perfect den, and many adults continue to use them throughout their lives.

Obviously you need to buy a crate that will be large enough to accommodate your GSP when he is fully grown. He needs space to stand up, turn around, and lie at full stretch, so a crate measuring 96cm high by 60cm by 68cm (38in x 24in x 27in) should be suitable for an average-sized German Shorthair.

You will also need to consider where you are going to locate the crate. The kitchen is usually the most suitable place as this is the hub of family life. Try to find a snug corner where the puppy can rest when he wants to, but where he can also see what is going on around him, and still be with the family.

Beds and bedding

The crate will need to be lined with bedding and the best type to buy is synthetic fleece. This is warm and cosy, and as moisture soaks through it, your puppy will not have a wet bed when he is tiny and is still unable to go through the night without relieving himself. This type of bedding is machine washable and easy to dry; buy two pieces, so you have one to use while the other piece is in the wash.

If you have purchased a crate, you may not feel the need to buy an extra bed, although many GSPs like to have a bed in the family room so they feel part of household activities. There is an amazing array of dog-beds to chose from – duvets, bean bags, cushions, baskets, igloos, mini-four posters – so you can take your pick! However, you do need to bear in mind that a GSP can be very destructive, so you would be advised to delay making a major investment until your puppy has gone through the worst of the chewing phase.

Collar and lead

You may think that it is not worth buying a collar for the first few weeks, but the sooner your pup gets used to it, the better. All you need is a lightweight collar to start with; you will need something more substantial as your GSP becomes bigger and stronger.

A German Shorthair puppy is always on the lookout for mischief!

A nylon lead is suitable for early lead training, as long as the fastening is secure. You will probably need a leather lead, with a trigger fastening, when your GSP is full grown, as nylon leads tend to chafe your hands.

ID

Your German Shorthair must wear some form of ID when he is out in public places – this is a legal requirement for all dogs. ID can be in form of a disk, engraved with your contact details, attached to the collar. When your GSP is full-grown, you can buy an embroidered collar with your contact details, which eliminates the danger of the disk becoming detached from the collar.

You may also wish to consider a permanent form of ID. Increasingly breeders are getting puppies microchipped before they go to their new homes. A microchip is the size of a grain of rice. It is 'injected' under the skin, usually between the shoulder blades, with a special needle. It has tiny barbs on it, which dig into the tissue around where it lies, so it does not migrate from that spot.

Each chip has its own unique identification number which can be read by a special scanner. That ID number is then registered on a national database with your name and details, so that if ever your dog

is lost, he can be taken to any vet or rescue centre where he is scanned and then you are contacted.

If your puppy has not been microchipped, you can ask your vet to do it, maybe when he goes along for his vaccinations.

Bowls

Your German Shorthair will need two bowls – one for food, and one for fresh drinking water, which should always be readily available. A stainless steel bowl is a good choice for a food bowl as it is tough and hygienic. Plastic bowls may be chewed, and there is a danger that bacteria can collect in the small cracks that may appear.

You can opt for a second stainless steel bowl for drinking water, or you may prefer a heavier ceramic bowl which will not be knocked over so easily.

Food

The breeder will let you know what your puppy is eating and should provide a full diet sheet to guide you through the first six months of your puppy's feeding regime – how much they are eating per meal, how many meals per day, when to increase the amounts given per meal and when to reduce the meals per day.

The breeder may provide you with some food when you go and collect your puppy, but it is worth making enquiries in advance about the availability of the brand that is recommended.

Grooming equipment

The German Shorthaired Pointer is low on maintenance as far as coat care is concerned, but a puppy needs to get used to being groomed and handled. To begin with, use a soft brush, and then invest in a good quality bristle brush when the adult coat comes through.

In addition you will need;

• Guillotine nail clippers

• Toothbrush (a finger brush is easiest to use) and specially manufactured dog toothpaste.

• Cotton-wool pads for cleaning the eyes and ears

Toys

German Shorthaired Pointers love to play. However, there are different schools of thought as to whether GSPs should have toys or not. Some of the diehard working people say no; they believe toys can make the dog hard mouthed or unsteady

If you are going to be using your GSP for gundog work, I would suggest that you don't play tugging games with raggers, as it could encourage him to do the same with game he is asked to retrieve in the future.

Gadgets that propel tennis balls are great fun for the dogs, but again, are not recommended if you plan to work your GSP as it could encourage him to chase game.

In my view your GSP puppy should have toys. Then it is up to you to train him and let him know what he can play with and what are training aids.

Our dogs have a variety of toys – rubber rings, balls and kongs; they do have raggers but we never play tug with them. However, they know that if the green canvas dummy comes out, it is training time. Dummies should never be used as toys. This is something that belongs to you, not the puppy, and you should only allow the puppy to use the dummy in a controlled environment under your terms.

Some dogs have one toy that lasts them a lifetime, but from experience this is rarely the case with a GSP; most soft plastic or fluffy toys soon get ripped to shreds. Your puppy should never be left to play with a new toy unattended. It is likely that he will chew it, which could be hazardous if he swallows part of it, which could result in choking or in a blockage, causing much distress to you and the puppy, not to mention a hefty vet bill.

If you have children, they must be taught to put their toys away when they have finished playing with them. A GSP does not know the difference between his toys and those belonging to the children, so there is every chance he will make the wrong choice, ruining the toy and possibly harming himself in the process.

I find the best toys for very young puppies are the cardboard inners of toilet rolls and kitchen towels. You may have a mess to clear up, but no damage is done.

The toys you buy must be suitably robust.

Finding a vet

Before your puppy arrives home, you should register with a vet. Visit vets in your local area, and speak to other pet owners that you might know, to see who they recommend. It is so important to find a good vet, almost as important as finding a good doctor for yourself. You need to find someone you can build up a good rapport with and have complete faith in. Word of mouth is really the best recommendation.

When you contact a veterinary practice, find out the following:

- Does the surgery run an appointment system?

- What are the arrangements for emergency, out of hours cover?

- Do any of the vets in the practice have experience treating German Shorthaired Pointers?

- What facilities are available at the practice?

If you are satisfied with what your find, and the staff appear to be helpful and friendly, book an appointment so your puppy can have a health check a couple of days after you collect him.

Settling in

When you first arrive home with your puppy, be careful not to overwhelm him. You and your family are hugely excited, but the puppy is in a completely strange environment with new sounds, smells and sights, which is a daunting experience, even for the boldest of pups.

Some puppies are very confident, wanting to play straightaway and quickly making friends; others need a little longer. Keep a close check on your GSP's body language and reactions so you can proceed at a pace he is comfortable with.

First, let him explore the garden. He will probably need to relieve himself after the journey home, so take him to the allocated toileting area and when he performs give him plenty of praise.

When you take your puppy indoors, let him investigate again. Show him his crate, and encourage him to go in by throwing in a treat. Let him have a sniff, and allow him to go in and out as he chooses. Later on, when he is tired, you can put him in the crate while you stay in the room. In this way he will learn to settle and will not think he is being abandoned.

It is a good idea to you feed your puppy in his crate, at least to begin with, as this helps to build up a positive association. It will not be long before your German Shorthair sees his crate as his own special den and will go there as a matter of choice. Some owners place a blanket over the crate, covering the back and sides, so that it is even more cosy and den-like.

Meeting the family

Resist the temptation of inviting friends and neighbours to come and meet the new arrival; your puppy needs to focus on getting to know his new family for the first few days. Try not to swamp your GSP with too much attention; give him a chance to explore and find his feet. There will be plenty of time for cuddles later on!

If you have children in the family, you need to keep everything as calm as possible. Your puppy may not have met children before, and even if he has, he will still find them strange and unpredictable. A puppy can become alarmed by too much noise, or he may go to the opposite extreme and become over-excited, which can lead to mouthing and nipping.

The best plan is to get the children to sit on the floor and give them all a treat. Each child can then call the puppy, stroke him, and offer a treat. In this way the puppy is making the decisions rather than being forced into interactions he may find stressful.

If he tries to nip or mouth, make sure there is a toy at the ready, so his attention can be diverted to something he is allowed to bite. If you do this consistently, he will learn to inhibit his desire to mouth when he is interacting with people.

Right from the start, impose a rule that the children are not allowed to pick up or carry the puppy. They can cuddle him when they are sitting on the floor. This may sound a little severe, but a wriggly puppy can be dropped in an instant, sometimes with disastrous consequences. If possible, try to make sure your GSP is only given attention when he has all four feet on the ground. This is a breed than can be boisterous, so it will pay dividends later on if your pup learns that jumping up is not rewarding.

Involve all family members with the day-to-day care of your puppy; this will enable the bond to develop with the whole family as opposed to just one person. Encourage the children to train and reward the puppy, teaching him to follow their commands without question.

The animal family

Care must be taken when introducing a puppy to a resident dog to ensure that relations get off on the right footing. German Shorthaired pointers enjoy the company of other dogs, so this is rarely a problem. However, it is inevitable that the older dog will feel a little threatened by the newcomer to begin with.

Your adult dog may be allowed to meet the puppy at the breeder's, which is ideal as the older dog will not feel territorial if he is away from home. But if this is not possible, allow your dog to smell the puppy's bedding (the bedding supplied by the breeder is fine) before they actually meet so he familiarises himself with the puppy's scent.

The garden is the best place for introducing the puppy, as the adult will regard it as neutral territory. He will probably take a great interest in the puppy and sniff him all over. Most puppies are naturally submissive in this situation, and your pup may lick the other dog's mouth or roll over on to his back. Try not to interfere as this is the natural way that dogs get to know each other.

You will only need to intervene if the older dog is too boisterous, and alarms the puppy. In this case, it is a good idea to put the adult on his lead so you have some measure of control.

It rarely takes long for an adult to accept a puppy, as he does not constitute a threat. This will be underlined if you make a big fuss of the older dog so that he has no reason to feel jealous. But no matter how well the two dogs are getting on, do not leave them alone unless one is crated.

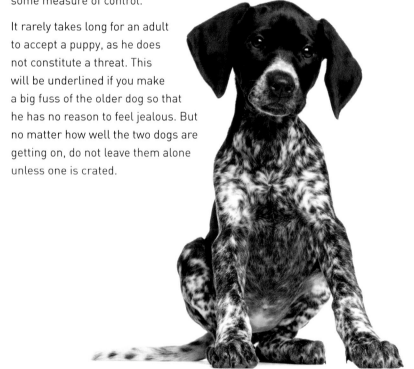

Feline freinds

A German Shorthaired Pointer will learn to live in harmony with the cat, but it is important to establish from an early stage that cats are not for chasing! You will need to work at early interactions and progress step by step, making sure they are never left alone together.

It may be easier if the cat is confined in a carrier for the first couple of meetings so your puppy has a chance to make acquaintance in a controlled situation. Keep calling your puppy to you and rewarding him so that he does not focus too intently on the cat. You can then graduate to holding your puppy while the cat is free, again rewarding him with a treat every time he responds to you and looks away from the cat. When you allow your puppy to go free, make sure the cat has an easy escape route, just in case he tries to chase.

This is an on-going process but, all the time your German Shorthair is learning that he is rewarded for ignoring the cat. In time, the novelty will wear off and the pair will live in harmony.

Feeding

The breeder will generally provide enough food for the first few days so the puppy does not have to cope with a change in diet – and possible digestive upset – along with all the stress of moving home.

Some puppies eat up their food from the first meal onwards, others are more concerned by their new surroundings and are too distracted to eat. Do not worry unduly if your puppy seems disinterested in his food for the first day or so. Give him 10 minutes to eat what he wants and then remove the leftovers and start afresh at the next meal. Obviously if you have any concerns about your puppy in the first few days, seek advice from your vet.

The German Shorthaired Pointer is keen on his food, so it is important that he learns food manners. He is not instinctively possessive about food, which is a trait that can be seen in some breeds, but he needs to know that you are in charge.

You can do this by giving your puppy half his ration, and then dropping food around his bowl. This will stop him guarding his bowl and, at the same time, he will see your presence in a positive light. You can also call him away from the bowl and reward him with some food – maybe something extra special – which he can take from your hand.

The first night

Your puppy will have spent the first weeks of his life either with his mother or curled up with his siblings. He is then taken from everything he knows as familiar, lavished with attention by his new family – and then comes bed time when he is left all alone. It is little wonder that he feels abandoned.

The best plan is to establish a night-time routine, and then stick to it so that your puppy knows what is expected of him. Take your puppy out into the garden to relieve himself, and then settle him in his crate. Some people leave a low light on for the puppy at night for the first week, others have tried a radio as company or a ticking clock. A covered hot-water bottle, filled with warm water, can also be a comfort. Like people, puppies are all individuals and what works for one, does not necessarily work for another, so it is a matter of trial and error.

Be very positive when you leave your puppy on his own; do not linger, or keep returning; this will make the situation more difficult. It is inevitable that he will protest to begin with, but if you stick to your routine, he will accept that he gets left at night – but you always return in the morning.

Rescued dogs

Settling an older, rescued dog in the home is very similar to a puppy in as much as you will need to make the same preparations regarding his homecoming. As with a puppy, an older dog will need you to be consistent, so start as you mean to go on.

There is often an initial honeymoon period when you bring a rescued dog home, where he will be on his best behaviour for the first few weeks. It is after these first couple of weeks that the true nature of the dog will show, so be prepared for subtle changes in his behaviour. It may be advisable to register with a reputable training club, so you can seek advice on any training or behavioural issues at an early stage.

Above all, remember that a rescued dog ceases to be a rescued dog the moment he enters his forever home and should be treated normally like any other family dog.

House training

New owners often dread this aspect of taking on a puppy, but if you work hard in the first few weeks, you will be amazed at how straightforward it can be.

The key to successful house training is vigilance and consistency. If you establish a routine, and you stick to it, your puppy will understand what is required. Equally, you must be there to supervise him at all times – except when he is safely tucked up in his crate. It is when a puppy is left to wander from room to room that accidents are most likely to happen.

As discussed earlier, you will have allocated a toileting area in your garden when preparing for your puppy's homecoming. You need to take your puppy to this area every time he needs to relieve himself so he builds up an association and knows why you have brought him out to the garden.

Establish a routine and make sure you take your puppy out at the following times:

- First thing in the morning
- After mealtimes
- On waking from a sleep
- Following a play session
- Last thing at night.

A puppy should be taken out to relieve himself every two hours as an absolute minimum. If you can manage an hourly trip out, so much the better. The more often your puppy gets it 'right', the quicker he will learn to be clean in the house. It helps if you use a verbal cue, such as "Busy", when your pup is performing and, in time, this will trigger the desired response.

Do not be tempted to put your puppy out on the doorstep in the hope that he will toilet on his own. Most pups simply sit there, waiting to get back inside the house! No matter how bad the weather is, accompany your puppy and give him lots of praise when he performs correctly.

Do not rush back inside as soon as he has finished, your puppy might start to delay in the hope of prolonging his time outside with you. Praise him, have a quick game – and then you can both return indoors.

When accidents happen

No matter how vigilant you are, there are bound to be accidents. If you witness the accident, take your puppy outside immediately, and give him lots of praise if he finishes his business out there.

If you are not there when he has an accident, do not scold him when you discover what has happened. He will not remember what he has done and will not understand why you are cross with him. Simply clean it up and resolve to be more vigilant next time.

Make sure you use a deodoriser (available in pet stores) when you clean up, otherwise your pup will be drawn to the smell and may be tempted to use the same spot again.

Vigilance is the key to successful house training.

Choosing a diet

There are so many different types of dog food on sale – all claiming to be the best – so how do you know what is likely to suit your German Shorthaired Pointer? This is an active dog that needs a well-balanced diet suited to his individual requirements.

When choosing a diet, there are basically three categories to choose from:

Complete

This is the most popular diet as it is easy to feed and is specially formulated with all the nutrients your dog needs. This means that you should not add any supplements or you may upset the nutritional balance.

Most complete diets come in different life stages: puppy, adult maintenance and senior, so this means that your GSP is getting what he needs when he is growing, during adulthood, and as he becomes older. You can even get prescription diets for dogs with particular health issues.

Generally, an adult maintenance diet should contain 21 to 24 per cent protein and 10 to 14 per cent fat. Protein levels should be higher in puppy diets, and reduced in veteran diets.

There are many different brands to choose from so seek advice from your puppy's breeder, who will have lengthy experience of feeding German Shorthaired Pointers.

Canned/pouches

This type of food is usually fed with hard biscuit, and most German Shorthairs find it very appetising. However, the ingredients – and the nutritional value – do vary significantly between different brands, so you will need to check the label. This type of food often has a high moisture content, so you need to be sure your GSP is getting sufficient nutrition.

Homemade

Some owners like to prepare meals especially for their dogs – and it is probably much appreciated. The danger is that although the food is tasty, and your GSP may enjoy the variety, you cannot be sure that it has the correct nutritional balance.

If this is a route you want to go down, you will need to find out the exact ratio of fats, carbohydrates, proteins, minerals and vitamins that are needed, which is quite an undertaking.

The Barf (Biologically Appropriate Raw Food) diet is another, more natural approach to feeding. Dogs are fed a diet mimicking what they would have eaten in the wild, consisting of raw meat, bone, muscle, fat, and vegetable matter. German Shorthaired Pointers appear to do well on this diet so it is certainly worth considering. There are now a number of companies that specialise in producing the Barf diet in frozen form, which will make your job a lot easier.

Feeding regime

When your puppy arrives in his new home he will need four meals, evenly spaced throughout the day. You may decide to keep to the diet recommended by your puppy's breeder, and if your pup is thriving there is no need to change. However, if your puppy is not doing well on the food, or you have problems with supply, you will need to make a change.

When switching diets, it is very important to do it on a gradual basis, changing over from one food to the next, a little at a time, and spreading the transition over a week to 10 days. This will avoid the risk of digestive upset.

When your puppy is around 12 weeks, you can cut out one of his meals; he may well have started to leave some of his food, indicating he is ready to do this. By six months he can move on to two meals a day – a regime that will suit him for the rest of his life.

A regime of two meals a day will suit most adults.

Bones and chews

Puppies love to chew, and many adults also enjoy gnawing on a bone. Bones should always be hard and uncooked; rib bones and poultry bones must be avoided as they can splinter and cause major problems. Dental chews, and some of the manufactured rawhide chews are safe, but they should only be given under supervision.

Ideal weight

In order to help to keep your German Shorthaired Pointer in good health it is necessary to monitor his weight. It is all too easy for the pounds to pile on, and this can result in serious health problems.

The major problem is feeding too much food in relation to the amount of energy your dog is expending. This is easily done if you follow feeding guidelines on packet foods, rather than monitoring your dog's individual weight and lifestyle.

It is easy to keep a check on a GSP's weight as he has no coat to disguise his figure! Make sure that when you look at your dog from above he has a definite 'waist'. You should be able to feel his ribs, but not see them.

In order to keep a close check on your GSP's weight, get into the habit of visiting your veterinary surgery on a monthly basis so that you can weigh him. You can keep a record of his weight so you can make adjustments if necessary.

If you are concerned that your GSP is putting on too much weight, consult your vet who will help you to plan a suitable diet.

Diet should be matched to your dog's energy output.

Caring for your GSP

The German Shorthaired Pointer is a breed without exaggeration. As a result he is relatively easy to care for. But, like all animals, a GSP has his own special needs which you must take on board.

Puppy grooming

For the most part, a German Shorthair puppy does not need very much coat care, but do not make the mistake of thinking the coat will take care of itself and never needs to be groomed. A grooming session is the best way to teach your puppy to accept all-over handling, which will prepare him for examinations by the vet and any other procedure that may be necessary.

Start by handling your puppy all over, stroking him from his head to his tail. Lift up each paw in turn, and reward him with a treat when he co-operates. Then roll him over on to his back and tickle his tummy; this is a very vulnerable position for a dog to adopt, so do not force the issue. Be firm but gentle, and give your puppy lots of praise when he does as you ask.

When your GSP is happy to be handled in this way, you can introduce a soft brush and spend a few minutes grooming the coat, and then reward him. In this way, he will gradually learn to accept the attention, and will relax while you groom him.

Adult grooming

An adult German Shorthaired Pointer has a dense wooly undercoat which protects him from the cold, and a short, water-resistant top coat which feels harsh to the touch. This is very easy to maintain with a bristle brush, which helps to get rid of superficial dirt.

Remember that even if the coat does not need to be brushed, the process of grooming acts as a massage which tones the muscles and aids circulation. A polish with a chamois leather will bring out the sheen in the coat, and this is the only extra attention that is needed when a German Shorthaired Pointer is exhibited in the show ring.

Your GSP will shed his coat, but because it is so short, you will not be swamped by dog hair! However, regular brushing while the coat is shedding will help to loosen the dead hairs and speed up the process.

Bathing is only needed on an occasional basis as the GSP tends to be low on dog odour. However there will, inevitably, be times when your GSP has decided to roll in something smelly, and you will have no option but to bath him For this reason, it is a good idea to bath your GSP before he needs it, so you can both get used to the procedure.

Routine care

In addition to grooming, you will need to carry out some routine care.

Eyes

The eyes should always be bright, with no trace of soreness or discharge. Occasionally, first thing in the morning, you may notice a small amount of discharge, which we call 'sleep dust'. This is nothing to worry about; just wipe it away using a damp cotton pad, making sure you use a separate pad for each eye.

However, if your GSP continually has discharge or watery eyes, or his eye look dull, you should consult your vet.

Ears

The ears should be clean and free from odour. You can buy specially-manufactured ear wipes, or you can use a cotton pad and an ear wash to clean them if necessary.

Dampen the pad with ear wash and gently wipe round the inside surface of the dog's ear.

Use a bristle brush to keep the coat in good order.

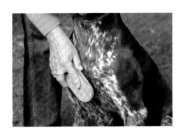

Do not probe too deeply when you clean the ears.

Regular teeth cleaning will prevent the build-up of tartar.

Trim nails little but often.

Try to reach the nooks and crannies, but do not poke deeper into the ear canal as you could cause damage. Allow your dog to shake off any excess moisture; this will help prevent infection.

Teeth

Dental disease is becoming more prevalent among dogs, so teeth cleaning should be seen as an essential part of your care regime. Look for warning signs of gum disease such as bad breath, red and swollen gums, a yellow-brown crust of tartar around the teeth, and pain or bleeding when you touch the gums or mouth. You should also watch for discoloured, fractured, or missing teeth. Any bumps or masses within the mouth should also by be checked your vet.

Regular teeth cleaning means that you will prevent problems arising, or, at the very least, you will spot trouble at an early stage and will be able to take the appropriate action. Bear in mind that if tartar is allowed to accumulate, there may be no option but to get it removed by a vet, which involves a general anaesthetic.

When your German Shorthaired Pointer is still a puppy accustom him to teeth cleaning so it becomes a matter of routine. Dog toothpaste comes in a variety of meaty flavours, which your GSP will like, so you can start by putting some toothpaste on your finger and gently rubbing his teeth. You can then progress to using a finger brush or a toothbrush, whichever you find most convenient.

Remember to reward your GSP when he co-operates and then he will positively look forward to his teeth-cleaning sessions.

Feet

Your GSP's feet need to be checked. Look for foreign objects, thorns, small stones, glass, etc. that could be stuck in his pads. Also look for cracks and small cuts that could become infected and make him lame. Check his nails for signs of damage or infection around the nail bed.

Nail trimming is a task dreaded by many owners – and many dogs – but, again, if you start early on, your GSP will get used to the procedure. Hopefully, the breeder will have started the process by trimming the puppies' nails when they are just a few weeks' old to stop them scratching their mother's underside when they are feeding.

If your dog has white nails, you will be able to see the quick (the vein that runs through the nail), which you must avoid at all costs. If you cut the quick it will bleed profusely and cause considerable discomfort. Obviously, the task is much harder in dark nails as you cannot see the quick. The best policy is to trim little and often so the nails don't grow too long, and you do not risk cutting too much and catching the quick.

If you are worried about trimming your GSP's nails, go to your vet so you can see it done properly. If you are still concerned, you can always use the services of a professional groomer.

Exercise

The German Shorthaired Pointer was bred to be an all purpose gundog, ready and able to work long, arduous days in the field. He is built on athletic line, and thrives on physical exercise. Although he has adapted brilliantly to being a companion dog, this

Most important of all, be guided by your German Shorthaired Pointer. He will have good days when he feels up to going for a walk, and other days when he would prefer to potter in the garden. If you have a younger dog at home, this may well stimulate your GSP to take more of an interest in what is going on, but make sure he is not pestered as he needs to rest undisturbed when he is tired.

Saying goodbye

It would be wonderful if dogs lived as long as humans; unfortunately they are with us for too short a time. Be it old age, illness or accident, losing a beloved companion is harrowing and, from experience, it never gets easier. No matter how many German Shorthaired Pointers you have owned, they are all special and it is heart wrenching to say goodbye.

We all hope that our best friend will die peacefully in his sleep, but sadly that rarely happens and you have to make the hard decision to have him put to sleep. One thing is for sure; it is the final act of love and kindness that you can give to a GSP who has given you so much, and it is only fair that he should be allowed to die with dignity.

There is never a right time, but you must put your feelings aside and do what is best for your German Shorthair. When the time comes, make the decision quickly and do not allow the dog to suffer. People ask me how do you know when it is time, especially if the dog is very ill or old and frail? For me, it is about quality of life and as long as the dog is not in pain, still eating, wags his tail and wants to go out, then it is OK to keep going.

GSPs are active dogs and it would not be right to keep one alive on drugs with no quality of life. I believe there comes a time when a German Shorthair has 'the' look in his eyes that seems to say: "I've had enough. Please help me." If you are in doubt, talk to your vet who will be able to make an objective assessment of your GSP's condition and will help you to make the right decision.

Should you be with your dog at the end? This is a personal choice, but for me it's a no brainer. I was there when the puppy was born and it is only right that I should be there when he passes on. It all happens quickly and is completely painless, albeit very upsetting for the owner.

This is the hardest thing you will ever have to do as a dog owner, and it is only natural to grieve for your beloved German Shorthaired Pointer. But eventually, you will be able to look back on the happy memories of times spent together, and this will bring much comfort. You may, in time, feel that your life is not complete without a German Shorthair, and you will feel ready to welcome a new puppy into your home.

Social skills

To live in the modern world, without fears and anxieties, your German Shorthaired Pointer needs to receive an education in social skills so that he learns to cope calmly and confidently in a wide variety of situations. The GSP has a sound temperament with no hang-ups, so if you spend time socialising him in his first 12 months, he will be set for life.

Early learning

The breeder will have begun a programme of socialisation by getting the puppies used to all the sights and sounds of a busy household. You need to continue this when your pup arrives in his new home, making sure he is not worried by household equipment, such as the vacuum cleaner or the washing machine, and that he gets used to unexpected noises from the radio and television.

As already highlighted, it is important that you handle your puppy on a regular basis so he will accept grooming and other routine care, and will not be worried if he has to be examined by the vet.

To begin with, your puppy needs to get used to all the members of his new family, but then you should give him the opportunity to meet friends and other people that come to the house. German Shorthairs are naturally friendly and outgoing, but sometimes their enthusiasm can get the better of them. A friendly greeting is one thing; being knocked for six is quite another! It is therefore important that your GSP learns appropriate greeting behaviour right from the start.

When visitors arrive at your home, adopt the following procedure:

- Make sure your GSP is on the lead so you are in control.

- When you go to the answer the door, make sure you have treats at the ready.

- Ask your GSP to "Sit" before opening the door, and reward him with a treat.

- When you open the door, make sure your GSP remains in the Sit, correcting him (and rewarding again) if necessary.

- The next step is to ask the visitor to give your GSP a treat, but makes sure he remains in the Sit.

This process is quite long-winded so the best plan is to practise with friends who are used to dogs until your German Shorthair understands what is required.

If you do not have children of your own, make sure your puppy has the chance to meet and play with other people's children so he learns that humans come in small sizes, too.

The outside world

When your puppy has completed his vaccinations, he is ready to venture into the outside world. In most cases a GSP puppy will take a lively interest in anything new and will relish the opportunity to broaden his horizons. However, there is a lot for a youngster to take on board, so do not swamp him with too many new experiences when you first set out.

The best plan is to start in a quiet area with light traffic, and only progress to a busier place when your puppy is ready. There is so much to see and hear – people (maybe carrying bags or umbrellas), pushchairs, bicycles, cars, lorries, machinery – so give your puppy a chance to take it all in.

If he does appear worried, do not fall into the trap of sympathizing with him, or worse still, picking him up. This will only teach your pup that he had a good reason to be worried and, with luck, you will 'rescue' him if he feels scared.

Instead, give a little space so he does not have to confront whatever he is frightened of, and distract him with a few treats. Then encourage him to walk past, using a calm, no-nonsense approach. Your pup will take the lead from you, and will realize there is nothing to fear.

Your pup also needs to continue his education in canine manners, started by his mother and by his littermates, as he needs to be able to greet all dogs calmly, giving the signals that say he is friendly and offers no threat. If you have a friend who has a dog of sound temperament, this is an ideal beginning. As your puppy gets older and more established, you can widen his circle of canine acquaintances.

Training classes

A training class will give your German Shorthaired Pointer the opportunity to work alongside other dogs in a controlled situation, and he will also learn to focus on you in a different, distracting environment. Both these lessons will be vital as your GSP matures.

However, the training class needs to be of the highest calibre, or you risk doing more harm than good. Before you go along with your puppy, attend a class as an observer to make sure you are happy with what goes on.

Find out the following:

- How much training experience do the instructors have?

- Are the classes divided into appropriate age categories?

- Do the instructors have experience training gundogs?

  - Do they use positive, reward-based training methods?

    If the training class is well run, it is certainly worth attending. Both you and your GSP will learn useful training exercises; it will increase his social skills, and you will have the chance to talk to lots of like-minded dog enthusiasts.

Training guidelines

We are fortunate that the German Shorthaired Pointer is a biddable dog and he likes to please his human family. He is highly intelligent and picks up new exercises quickly, so your job is to provide lots of mental stimulation!

You will be keen to get started, but in your rush to get training underway, do not neglect the fundamentals which could make the difference between success and failure.

When you start training, try to observe the following guidelines:

- Choose an area that is free from distractions so your puppy will focus on you. You can progress to a more challenging environment as your pup progresses.

- Do not train your puppy just after he has eaten

or when you have returned from exercise. He will either be too full, or too tired, to concentrate.

- Do not train if you are in a bad mood, or if you are short of time – these sessions always end in disaster!

- Make sure you have a reward your GSP values – tasty treats, such as cheese or cooked liver, or an extra special toy.

- If you are using treats, make sure they are bite-size, otherwise you will lose momentum when your pup stops to chew on his treat.

- Keep your verbal cues simple, and always use the same one for each exercise. For example, when you ask your puppy to go into the Down position, the cue is "Down", not "Lie Down", "Get Down", or anything else... Remember your GSP does not speak English; he associates the sound of the word with the action.

- If your GSP is finding an exercise difficult, break it down into small steps so it is easier to understand.

- Do not make your training sessions boring and repetitious; your GSP will quickly lose interest and he may cease to co-operate.

- Do not train for too long, particularly with a young puppy who has a very short attention span, and always end training sessions on a positive note.

- Above all, have fun so you and your GSP both enjoy spending quality time together.

Training sessions should be fun for both of you.

First lessons

A young German Shorthaired Pointer will soak up new experiences like a sponge, so training should start from the time your pup arrives in his new home. It is so much easier to teach good habits rather than trying to correct your puppy when he has established an undesirable pattern of behaviour.

Wearing a collar

You may, or may not, want your German Shorthair to wear a collar all the time. But when he goes out in public places he will need to be on a lead, and so he should be used to the feel of a collar around his neck. The best plan is to accustom your pup to wearing a soft collar for a few minutes at a time until he gets used to it.

Fit the collar so that you can get at least two fingers between the collar and his neck. Then have a game to distract his attention. This will work for a few moments; then he will stop, put his back leg up behind his neck and

scratch away at the peculiar itchy thing round his neck, which feels so odd.

Bend down, rotate the collar, pat him on the head and distract him by playing with a toy or giving him a treat. Once he has worn the collar for a few minutes each day, he will soon ignore it and become used to it.

Remember, never leave the collar on the puppy unsupervised, especially when he is outside in the garden, or when he is in his crate, as it could get snagged, causing serious injury.

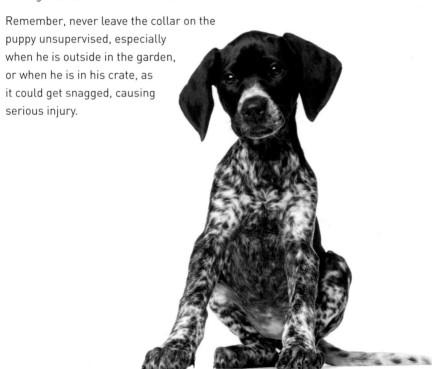

Walking on the lead

This sounds easy, but it is an exercise that frustrates many owners. The German Shorthaired Pointer does not see the point in hanging around, or taking things at a steady pace. He wants to get going, now!

There is no denying that German Shorthairs do tend to pull on the lead, so the sooner you start working on this lesson – making sure you give lots of rewards for the behaviour you want – the greater your chances of success will be.

- Once your puppy is used to the collar, take him outside into your secure garden where there are no distractions.

- Attach the lead and, to begin with, allow him to wander with the lead trailing, making sure it does not become snagged up. Then pick up the lead and follow the pup where he wants to go; he needs to get used to the sensation of being attached to you.

- The next stage is to get your GSP to follow you, and for this you will need some tasty treats. You can show him a treat in your hand, and then encourage him to follow you. Walk a few paces, and if he is co-operating, stop and reward him. If he puts on the brakes, simply change direction and lure him with the treat.

- Next introduce some changes of direction so your puppy is walking confidently alongside you. At this stage, introduce a verbal cue "Heel" when your puppy is in the correct position.

- You can then graduate to walking your puppy outside the home – as long as he has completed his vaccination programme – starting in quiet areas and building up to busier environments.

Do not expect too much of your puppy too soon when you are lead walking away from home. He will be distracted by the new sights and sounds he encounters, so concentrating on lead training will be difficult for him. Give him a chance to look and see, and reward him frequently when he is walking forward confidently on a loose lead.

Be prepared to spend a considerable amount of time to establish good lead-walking as it will have far-reaching effects. A German Shorthair that pulls on the lead is a nightmare to live with, and you will soon start excluding him from expeditions on which you know he will be a problem. However, if your GSP is trained to walk calmly beside you, on a loose lead, he will become your constant companion, and will be a pleasure to own.

The aim is for your German Shorthair to walk on a loose lead – neither pulling ahead nor lagging behind.

Come when called

The German Shorthaired Pointer is an energetic dog who loves the opportunity to free run and to investigate all the fascinating smells he comes across. You can only allow your dog this type of freedom if he has a reliable recall.

The German Shorthair is a people-orientated dog and, in most cases, he will not stray too far away and will be happy to come back to you. However, there will be times when he finds a scent and you find he has developed selective hearing.

The key to successful recall training is to start early. Hopefully, the breeder will have laid the foundations by calling the puppies to "Come" when it is feeding time, or when moving from one place to another.

You can build on this when your puppy arrives in his new home, calling him to "Come" when he is in a confined space, such as the kitchen. This is a good place to build up a positive association with the verbal cue – particularly if you ask your puppy to "Come" to get his dinner!

The next stage is to transfer the lesson to the garden. Arm yourself with some treats, and wait until your puppy is distracted. Then call him, using a higher-pitched, excited tone of voice. At this stage, a puppy wants to be with you, so capitalise on this and keep practising the verbal cue, rewarding your puppy with a treat and praise when he comes to you.

Now you are ready to introduce some distractions. Try calling him when someone else is in the garden, or wait a few minutes until he is investigating a really interesting scent. When he responds, make a really big fuss of him and give him extra treats so he knows it is worth his while to come to you. If your puppy responds, immediately reward him with a treat.

If he is slow to come, run away a few steps and then call again, making yourself sound really exciting. Jump up and down, and open your arms wide to welcome him; it doesn't matter how silly you look, he needs to see you as the most fun person in the world.

When you have a reliable recall in the garden, you can venture into the outside world. Do not be too ambitious to begin with; try a recall in a quiet place with the minimum of distractions.

Do not make the mistake of only asking your dog to come at the end of his allotted exercise period. What is the incentive in coming back to you if all you do is clip on his lead, marking the end of his free time? Instead, call your dog at random times, giving him a treat and a stroke, and then letting him go free again.

Stationary exercises

The Sit and Down are easy to teach, and mastering these exercises will be rewarding for both you and your German Shorthaired Pointer.

Sit

The best method is to lure your GSP into position, and for this you can use a treat, a toy, or his food bowl.

- Hold the reward (a treat or food bowl) above his head. As he looks up, he will lower his hindquarters and go into a sit.

- Practise this a few times and when your puppy understands what you are asking, introduce the verbal cue, "Sit".

When your GSP understands the exercise, he will respond to the verbal cue alone, and you will not need to reward him every time he sits. However, it is a good idea to give him a treat on a random basis when he co-operates to keep him guessing!

Down

This is an important lesson, and can be a lifesaver if an emergency arises and you need to bring your German Shorthair to an instant halt.

You can start with your dog in a Sit or a Stand for this exercise. Stand or kneel in front of him and show him you have a treat in your hand. Hold the treat just in front of his nose and slowly lower it towards the ground, between his front legs.

As your GSP follows the treat he will go down on his front legs and, in a few moments, his hindquarters will follow. Close your hand over the treat so he doesn't cheat and get the treat before he is in the correct position. As soon as he is in the Down, give him the treat and lots of praise.

Keep practising, and when your GSP understands what you want, introduce the verbal cue "Down".

Control exercises

These exercises are not the most exciting, particularly for a German Shorthaired Pointer who likes to be on the go. However, they are useful in a variety of different situations. They teach your GSP that you are someone to be respected. He will learn that provided he co-operates, he will be rewarded for making the right decision.

Wait

This exercise teaches your German Shorthair to "Wait" in position until you give the next command; it differs from the Stay exercise where he must stay where you have left him for a more prolonged period. The most useful application of "Wait" is when you are getting your dog out of the car and you need him to stay in position until you clip on his lead.

Start with your puppy on the lead to give you a greater chance of success. Ask him to "Sit", and stand in front him. Step back one pace, holding your hand, palm flat, facing him. Wait a second and then come back to stand in front of him again. You can then reward him and release him with a word, such as "OK".

Practise this a few times, waiting a little longer before you reward him, and then introduce the verbal cue "Wait".

You can reinforce the lesson by using it in different situations, such as asking your GSP to "Wait" before you put his food bowl down.

Stay

You need to differentiate this exercise from the Wait by using a different hand signal and a different verbal cue.

- Start with your GSP in the Down as he is most likely to be secure in this position. Stand by his side and then step forwards, with your hand held back, palm facing the dog.

- Step back, release him, and then reward him. Practise until your GSP understands the exercise and then introduce the verbal cue "Stay".

- Gradually increase the distance you can leave your puppy, and increase the challenge by walking around him – and even stepping over him – so that he learns he must "Stay" until you release him.

Leave

A response to this verbal cue means that your German Shorthaired Pointer will learn to give up a toy on request, and it follows on that he will give up anything when he is asked, which is very useful if he has got hold of a forbidden object. You can also use it if you catch him red-handed raiding the bin, or stealing food from a kitchen surface, which is a GSP speciality!

- The "Leave" command can be taught quite easily when you are first playing with your puppy. As you gently take a toy from his mouth, introduce the verbal cue, "Leave", and then praise him.

- If he is reluctant, swap the toy for another toy or a treat. This will usually do the trick.

- Do not try to pull the toy from his mouth if he refuses to give it up, as this will only make him keener to hang on to it. Let the toy go 'dead' in your hand, and then swap it for a new, exciting toy, so this becomes the better option.

- Remember to make a big fuss of your GSP when he co-operates. If he is rewarded with verbal praise, plus a game with a toy or a tasty treat, he will learn that "Leave" is always a good option.

Be ready to reward
your German Shorthair
for making the 'right'
decision.

Opportunities
for GSPs

The German Shorthaired Pointer thrives on mental stimulation. He is a natural all-rounder and will excel in many of the sports and disciplines.

Good citizen scheme

The Kennel Club Good Citizen Scheme was introduced to promote responsible dog ownership, and to teach dogs basic good manners. In the US there is one test; in the UK there are four award levels: Puppy Foundation, Bronze, Silver and Gold.

Exercises within the scheme include:

- Walking on lead

- Road walking

- Control at door/gate.

- Food manners

- Recall

- Stay

- Send to bed

- Emergency stop.

Obedience

If your German Shorthaired Pointer has mastered basic obedience, you may want to get involved in competitive obedience. The exercises include heelwork at varying paces with dog and handler following a pattern decided by the judge, stays, recalls, retrieves, sendaways, scent discrimination and distance control. The exercises get progressively harder as you progress up the classes.

Rally O

If you do not want to get involved in the rigours of Competitive Obedience, you may find that a sport called Rally O is more to your liking.

This is loosely based on Obedience, and also has a few exercises borrowed from Agility when you get to the highest levels. Handler and dog must complete a course, in order, which has a variety of between 12 and 20 different exercises. The course is timed and the team must complete within the time limit that is set, but there are no bonus marks for speed.

The great advantage of Rally O is that it is very relaxed, and anyone can compete; indeed, it has proved very popular for handlers with disabilities, as they are able to work their dogs to a high standard and compete on equal terms with other competitors.

Agility

In this sport, the dog completes an obstacle course under the guidance of his owner. You need a good element of control, as the dog completes the course off the lead.

In competition, each dog completes the course individually and is assessed on both time and accuracy. The dog that completes the course with the fewest faults, in the fastest time, wins the class. The obstacles include an A-frame, a dog-walk, weaving poles, a see-saw, tunnels, and jumps.

Field trials

These are highly competitive, sometimes arduous, events over rough territory, held under national Kennel Club rules to resemble a day's shooting in the field. Field trial GSPs are expected to work with all manner of game – rabbits and hares, partridges and pheasants in the UK; quail, pheasant, grouse and partridge in the USA, and display their hunting ability and their obedience to commands.

Hunting tests

These are run in the USA and are on similar lines to Field Trials, except dogs are measured against a set standard rather than as a competition between dogs. There are three levels: Junior, Senior and Master.

Working tests

Similar to field trials and held in the summer months in the UK, the work here is based on canvas dummies. You and your GSP will be required to complete several tests including hunting, retrieving and a retrieve from water. These are great fun days out and a good test of your training.

Canicross

This is a relatively new sport and it is tailor-made for fit owners who have dogs with high exercise requirements. Basically, it involves cross country running attached to your dog. You will need some specialised equipment (a belt for you and a bungee-style line for your GSP). Dogs must be 12 months old to compete, but you can start fitness training from around nine months and also teach all-important instructions, such as "haw" (left), "gee" (right), "steady" and "whoa".

Showing

Exhibiting a dog in the show ring entails a lot of training and preparation. Your German Shorthaired Pointer needs to remain calm in the busy show atmosphere, so you need to work on his socialisation, and then take him to ringcraft classes so you both learn what is required in the ring.

Your GSP will be subjected to a detailed 'hands on'

examination by the judge; he will need to stand still in a show pose and will also need to move on a loose lead so the judge can assess his gait.

Showing at the top level is highly addictive, so watch out – once you start, you will never have a free date in your diary!

Flyball

Flyball is a team sport; the dogs love it and it is undoubtedly the noisiest of all the canine sports!

Four dogs are selected to run in a relay race against an opposing team. The dogs are sent out by their handlers to jump four hurdles, catch the ball from the flyball box and then return over the hurdles. At the top level, this sport is fast and furious and although it is dominated by Border Collies, the GSP can make a big contribution.

Tracking

The German Shorthaired Pointer, with his outstanding sense of smell, is a good choice for this demanding sport in which the dog must learn to follow scent trails of varying age, over different types of terrain. In the US, this is a sport in its own right; in the UK it is incorporated into Working Trials where a dog must also compete in two other elements – control and agility.

Health care

We are fortunate that the German Shorthaired Pointer is a healthy dog and, with good routine care, a well-balanced diet, and sufficient exercise, most will experience few health problems.

However, it is your responsibility to put a programme of preventative health care in place – and this should start from the moment your puppy, or older dog, arrives in his new home.

Vaccinations

Dogs are subject to a number of contagious diseases. In the past, these were killers, and resulted in heartbreak for many owners. Vaccinations have now been developed, and the occurrence of the major infectious diseases is now very rare. However, this will only remain the case if all pet owners follow a strict policy of vaccinating their dogs.

There are vaccinations available for the following diseases:

Adenovirus: (Canine Adenovirus): This affects the liver; affected dogs have a classic 'blue eye'.

Distemper: A viral disease which causes chest and gastro-intestinal damage. The brain may also be affected, leading to fits and paralysis.

Parvovirus: Causes severe gastro enteritis, and most commonly affects puppies.

Leptospirosis: This bacterial disease is carried by rats and affects many mammals, including humans. It causes liver and kidney damage.

Rabies: A virus that affects the nervous system and is invariably fatal. The first signs are abnormal behaviour when the infected dog may bite another animal or a person. Paralysis and death follow. Vaccination is compulsory in most countries. In the UK, dogs traveling overseas must be vaccinated.

Kennel Cough: There are several strains of Kennel Cough, but they all result in a harsh, dry, cough. This disease is rarely fatal; in fact most dogs make a good recovery within a matter of weeks and show few signs of ill health while they are affected. However, kennel cough is highly infectious among dogs that live together so, for this reason, most boarding kennels will insist that your dog is protected by the vaccine, which is given as nose drops.

Lyme Disease: This is a bacterial disease transmitted by ticks (see page 170). The first signs are limping, but the heart, kidneys and nervous system can also be affected. The ticks that transmit the disease occur in specific regions, such as the north-east states of the USA, some of the southern states, California and the upper Mississippi region. Lyme disease is still rare in the UK so vaccinations are not routinely offered.

Vaccination programme

In the USA, the American Animal Hospital Association advises vaccination for core diseases, which they list as: distemper, adenovirus, parvovirus and rabies. The requirement for vaccinating for non-core diseases – leptospriosis, lyme disease and kennel cough – should be assessed depending on a dog's individual risk and his likely exposure to the disease.

In the UK, vaccinations are routinely given for distemper, adenovirus, leptospirosis and parvovirus.

In most cases, a puppy will start his vaccinations at around eight weeks of age, with the second part given a fortnight later. However, this does vary depending on the individual policy of veterinary practices, and the incidence of disease in your area. You should also talk to your vet about whether to give annual booster vaccinations. This depends on an individual dog's levels of immunity, and how long a particular vaccine remains effective.

Parasites

No matter how well you look after your German Shorthaired Pointer, you will have to accept that parasites – internal and external – are ever present, and you need to take preventative action.

Internal parasites: As the name suggests, these parasites live inside your dog. Most will find a home in the digestive tract, but there is also a parasite that lives in the heart. If infestation is unchecked, a dog's health will be severely jeopardised, but routine preventative treatment is simple and effective.

External parasites: These parasites live on your dog's body – in his skin and fur, and sometimes in his ears.

Roundworm

This is found in the small intestine, and signs of infestation will be a poor coat, a pot belly, diarrhoea and lethargy. Pregnant mothers should be treated,

but it is almost inevitable that parasites will be passed on to the puppies. For this reason, a breeder will start a worming programme, which you will need to continue. Ask your vet for advice on treatment, which should carry on throughout your dog's life.

Tapeworm

Infection occurs when fleas and lice are ingested; the adult worm takes up residence in the small intestine, releasing mobile segments (which contain eggs) that can be seen in a dog's faeces as small rice-like grains. The only other obvious sign of infestation is irritation of the anus. Again, routine preventative treatment is required throughout your GSP's life.

Heartworm

This parasite is transmitted by mosquitoes, and so will only occur where these insects thrive. A warm environment is needed for the parasite to develop, so it is more likely to be present in areas with a warm, humid climate. However, it is found in all parts of the USA, although its prevalence does vary. At present, heartworm is rarely seen in the UK.

Heartworm live in the right side of the heart. Larvae can grow up to 14in (35.5cm) in length. A dog with heartworm is at severe risk from heart failure, so preventative treatment, as advised by your vet, is essential. Dogs living in the USA should have regular blood tests to check for the presence of infection.

Lungworm

Lungworm, or *Angiostrongylus vasorum*, is a parasite that lives in the heart and major blood vessels supplying the lungs. It can cause many problems, such as breathing difficulties, blood-clotting problems, sickness and diarrhoea, seizures, and can even be fatal. The parasite is carried by slugs and snails, and the dog becomes infected when ingesting these, often accidentally when rummaging through undergrowth. Lungworm is not common, but it is on the increase and a responsible owner should be aware of it. Fortunately, it is easily preventable and even affected dogs usually make a full recovery if treated early enough. Your vet will be able to advise you on the risks in your area and what form of treatment may be required.

Fleas

A dog may carry dog fleas, cat fleas, and even human fleas. The flea stays on the dog only long enough to have a blood meal and to breed, but its presence will result in itching and scratching. If your dog has an allergy to fleas – which is usually a reaction to the flea's saliva – he will scratch himself until he is raw.

Spot-on treatment is easy to use and highly effective. You can also treat your dog with a spray or with insecticidal shampoo. Bear in mind that the whole environment and all other pets will need to be treated as well.

How to detect fleas

You may suspect your dog has fleas, but how can you be sure? There are two methods to try.

Run a fine comb through your dog's coat, and see if you can detect the presence of fleas on the skin, or clinging to the comb. Alternatively, sit your dog on some white paper and rub his back. This will dislodge faeces from the fleas, which will be visible as small brown specks. To double check, shake the specks on to some damp cotton-wool (cotton). Flea faeces consists of the dried blood taken from the host, so if the specks turn a lighter shade of red, you know your dog has fleas.

Ticks

These are blood-sucking parasites which are most frequently found in rural areas where sheep or deer are present. The main danger is their ability to pass lyme disease to both dogs and humans. Lyme disease is prevalent in some areas of the USA (see page 165), although it is still rare in the UK. The treatment you give your dog for fleas generally works for ticks, but you should discuss the best product to use with your vet.

How to remove a tick

If you spot a tick on your dog, do not try to pluck it off as you risk leaving the hard mouth parts embedded in his skin. The best way to remove a tick is to use a fine pair of tweezers or you can buy a tick remover. Grasp the tick head firmly and then pull the tick straight out from the skin. If you are using a tick remover, check the instructions, as some recommend a circular twist when pulling. When you have removed the tick, clean the area with mild soap and water.

Ear mites

These parasites live in the outer ear canal. The signs of infestation are a brown, waxy discharge, and your dog will continually shake his head and scratch his ear. If you suspect your German Shorthair has ear mites, a visit to the vet will be needed so that medicated ear drops can be prescribed.

Fur mites

These small, white parasites are visible to the naked eye and are often referred to as 'walking dandruff'. They cause a scurfy coat and mild itchiness. However, they are zoonetic – transferable to humans – so prompt treatment with an insecticide prescribed by your vet is essential.

Harvest mites

These are picked up from the undergrowth, and can be seen as a bright orange patch on the webbing between the toes, although this can be found elsewhere on the body, such as on the ears flaps. Treatment is effective with the appropriate insecticide.

Skin mites

There are two types of parasite that burrow into a dog's skin. *Demodex canis* is transferred from a mother to her pups while they are feeding. Treatment is with a topical preparation, and sometimes antibiotics are needed.

The other skin mite is *Sarcoptes scabiei*, which causes intense itching and hair loss. It is highly contagious, so all dogs in a household will need to be treated, which involves repeated bathing with a medicated shampoo.

Common ailments

As with all living animals, dogs can be affected by a variety of ailments. Most can be treated effectively after consulting with your vet, who will prescribe appropriate medication and will advise you on how to care for your dog's needs.

Here are some of the more common problems that could affect your German Shorthaired Pointer, with advice on how to deal with them.

Anal glands

These are two small sacs on either side of the anus, which produce a dark-brown secretion that dogs use when they mark their territory. The anal glands should empty every time a dog defecates, but if they become blocked or impacted, a dog will experience increasing discomfort. He may nibble at his rear end, or 'scoot' his bottom along the ground to relieve the irritation.

Treatment involves a trip to the vet, who will empty the glands manually. It is important to do this without delay or infection may occur.

Dental problems

Good dental hygiene will do much to minimise gum infection and tooth decay. If tartar accumulates to the extent that you cannot remove it by brushing, the vet will need to intervene. In a situation such as this, an anaesthetic will need to be administered so the tartar can be removed manually.

Diarrhoea

There are many reasons why a dog has diarrhoea, but most commonly it is the result of scavenging, a sudden change of diet, or an adverse reaction to a particular type of food.

If your dog is suffering from diarrhoea, the first step is to withdraw food for a day. It is important that he does not dehydrate, so make sure that fresh drinking water is available. However, drinking too much can increase the diarrhoea, which may be accompanied with vomiting, so limit how much he drinks at any one time.

After allowing the stomach to rest, feed a bland diet, such as white fish or chicken, with boiled rice for a few days. In most cases, your dog's motions will return to normal and you can resume usual feeding, although this should be done gradually.

However, if this fails to work and the diarrhoea persists for more than a few days, you should consult you vet. Your dog may have an infection which needs to be treated with antibiotics, or the diarrhoea may indicate some other problem which needs expert diagnosis.

Ear infections

The German Shorthaired Pointer has drop ears which lie close to his head, which increases the risk of ear infections.

A healthy ear is clean with no sign of redness or inflammation, and no evidence of a waxy brown discharge or a foul odour. If you see your dog scratching his ear, shaking his head, or holding one ear at an odd angle, you will need to consult your vet.

The most likely causes are ear mites, an infection, or there may a foreign body, such as a grass seed, trapped in the ear.

Depending on the cause, treatment is with medicated ear drops, possibly containing antibiotics. If a foreign body is suspected, the vet will need to carry our further investigations.

Eye problems

The German Shorthaired Pointer has medium-sized eyes that do not bulge, which would make them vulnerable to injury.

If your GSP's eyes look red and sore, he may be suffering from conjunctivitis. This may, or may not be accompanied with a watery or a crusty discharge. Conjunctivitis can be caused by a bacterial or viral infection, it could be the result of an injury, or it could be an adverse reaction to pollen.

You will need to consult your vet for a correct diagnosis, but in the case of an infection, treatment with medicated eye drops is effective.

Conjunctivitis may also be the first sign of more

serious inherited eye problems (see page 188).

In some instances, a dog may suffer from dry, itchy eye, which your dog may further injure through scratching. This condition, known as keratoconjunctivitis sicca, may be inherited.

Foreign bodies

In the home, puppies – and some older dogs – cannot resist chewing anything that looks interesting. The toys you choose for your dog should be suitably robust to withstand damage, but children's toys can be irresistible. Some dogs will chew – and swallow – anything from socks, tights, and any other items from the laundry basket to golf balls and stones from the garden. Obviously, these items are indigestible and could cause an obstruction in your dog's intestine, which is potentially lethal.

The signs to look for are vomiting, and a tucked up posture. The dog will often be restless and will look as though he is in pain.

In this situation, you must get your dog to the vet without delay as surgery will be needed to remove the obstruction.

Heatstroke

The German Shorthaired Pointer's head structure is without exaggeration, which means that he has a straightforward respiratory system.

However, all dogs are vulnerable to overheating in hot weather. If the weather is warm make sure your GSP always has access to shady areas, and wait for a cooler part of the day before going for a walk. Be extra careful if you leave your GSP in the car, as the temperature can rise dramatically - even on a cloudy day. Heatstroke can happen very rapidly, and unless you are able lower your dog's temperature, it can be fatal.

If your GSP appears to be suffering from heatstroke, lie him flat and work at lowering his temperature by spraying him with cool water and covering him with wet towels. As soon as he has made some recovery, take him to the vet, where cold intravenous fluids can be administered.

Lameness/limping

There are a wide variety of reasons why a dog can go lame. from a simple muscle strain to a fracture, ligament damage, or more complex problems with the joints. If you are concerned about your dog, do not delay in seeking help.

As your German Shorthaired Pointer becomes more elderly, he may suffer from arthritis, which you will see as general stiffness, particularly when he gets up after resting. It will help if you ensure his bed is in a warm draught-free location, and if your GSP gets wet after exercise, you must dry him thoroughly.

If you GSP seems to be in pain, consult your vet who will be able to help with pain relief medication.

Skin problems

If your dog is scratching or nibbling at his skin, first check he is free from fleas (see page 170). There are other external parasites which cause itching and hair loss, but you will need a vet to help you find the culprit.

An allergic reaction can cause major skin problems, but it can be quite an undertaking to find the cause of the allergy. You will need to follow your vet's advice, which often requires eliminating specific ingredients from the diet, as well as looking at environmental factors.

Breed-specific disorders

Like all pedigree dogs, the German Shorthaired Pointer does have a few breed-related disorders. If diagnosed with any of the diseases listed below, it is important to remember that they can affect offspring so breeding from affected dogs should be discouraged.

There are now recognised screening tests to enable breeders to check for affected individuals and reduce the prevalence of these diseases within the breed.

DNA testing is also becoming more widely available, and as research into the different genetic diseases progresses, more DNA tests are being developed.

Acral mutilation syndrome

This distressing disorder develops after birth as a result of abnormal development and degeneration of the neurons providing sensation to the paws. From approximately three months of age, affected puppies lick, bite and chew at their paws, causing themselves extensive damage yet continuing to walk about because of the loss of pain and temperature sensation in their paws. There is no effective treatment – sadly, euthanasia is a common outcome.

Aortic stenosis

This is a congenital malformation of the aorta, the major outflow vessel from the heart. The degree of stenosis or narrowing will determine how much harder the heart must work to pump blood out to the rest of the body and therefore how much the puppy is affected.

At its mildest, there may be no signs, with a murmur detected by a vet at a routine examination of the puppy but disappearing by six months of age. More severe narrowing may manifest as reduced exercise tolerance and fainting, or as overt left-sided heart failure with coughing and difficulty breathing.

Epilepsy

This is a condition caused by abnormal electrical activity in the brain. An affected dog is subject to sudden, uncontrolled physical fits that can last for a couple of minutes, during which time the dog may loose consciousness. Generally it manifests between the ages of nine months up to about three years. If it occurs in older dogs it can be a sign of other problems. Medication can control the condition but, unfortunately, there is no cure.

Gastric Dilatation-volvulus (GDV)

Commonly known as gastric torsion or bloat, this is a life-threatening condition that requires immediate urgent veterinary intervention. Time is critical and, sadly, even with immediate treatment, approximately 25-40 per cent of dogs do not recover.

When it occurs, the dog's stomach fills with air, fluid and/or food. The enlarged stomach places pressure on other organs and the stomach can twist which causes difficulty breathing, and a decrease in blood supply to the dog's vital organs. General symptoms include: a distended abdomen, unsuccessful attempts to belch or vomit, retching without producing anything, weakness, excessive salivation, shortness of breath, cold body temperature, pale gums, rapid heartbeat and collapse.

Hemivertebrae

The vertebrae are the building blocks of the spine, designed to protect the spinal cord. Hemivertebrae are mis-shapen, wedge-shaped deformed vertebrae whose protective role is therefore compromised.

In the GSP, the thoracic vertebrae are occasionally affected. Effects on the individual will be determined by the nature of the deformity, with kyphosis or kinking of the vertebral column, spinal cord compression, hindlimb weakness and pain, and at worst resulting in paralysis. Surgery may be possible but needs careful pre-operative evaluation.

Hip dysplasia (HD)

This is where the ball-and-socket joint of the hip develops incorrectly so that the head of the femur (ball) and the acetabulum of the pelvis (socket) do not fit snugly. This causes pain in the joint and may be seen as lameness in dogs as young as five months old with deterioration into severe arthritis over time. In the US, hip scoring is carried out by the Orthopaedic Foundation for Animals. X-rays are submitted when a dog is two years old, categorised as Normal (Excellent, Good, Fair), Borderline, and Dysplastic (Mild, Moderate, Severe). The hip grades of Excellent, Good and Fair are within normal limits and are given OFA numbers.

In the UK, the minimum age for the hips to be assessed by X-ray is 12 months. Each hip can score from a possible perfect 0 to a deformed 53. Both left and right scores are added together to give the total hip score.

Lupoid dermatosis

From six months of age, there is thickening, scaling and crusting of the skin, initially affecting the head, legs and scrotum (in male dogs) and gradually spreading, or there may be a waxing and waning pattern. Affected areas may be painful or itchy. Nails may fall out, and there may be fever. Diagnosis is based on a skin biopsy. There is no specific treatment available yet. Shampoos, corticosteroids and fatty acid supplements may help.

Ocular conditions

Entropion is an inrolling of the eyelids, occasionally
affecting the outer parts of the lower eyelids in the GSP.
There are degrees of entropion, ranging from a slight
inrolling to the more serious case, requiring surgical
correction because of the pain and damage to the
surface of the eyeball.

There is a breed predisposition to eversion of the
cartilage of the nictitating membrane, where the edge of
the third eyelid is rolled outwards. Resultant irritation to
the eye may be mild or severe enough to require surgery.

A cataract is a cloudiness of the lens of the eye. A
developmental form of hereditary cataract occurs rarely
in the young GSP from 6 to 18 months of age (in contrast
to the congenital form seen in other breeds where some
form of lens opacity is present from birth).

A late-onset form of generalised progressive retinal
atrophy is a rare condition in the GSP.

Von willebrand's disease

This rare bleeding disorder results in a tendency to bleed
easily, and should be suspected if there is prolonged
bleeding after an injury or surgery, bleeding from the
nose/gums, or if blood is seen in the urine. Affected
individuals can lead normal lives, although special
care must be taken to avoid inadvertent injuries around

the house by applying padding to sharp corners, and when clipping the coat and claws, for example. It can be diagnosed with blood tests, and DNA testing is available.

XX sex reversal

The sex of a puppy is determined by the inheritance of a Y or X chromosome from the sire. Rarely, a puppy with XX chromosomes – who therefore should be female – may have the gonads of a male (testicles) and female (ovaries) (i.e. hermaphrodite), or just male gonads. This is a very rare condition in the GSP, manifesting as infertility and abnormal or unexpected external genitalia.

Summing up

It may be a cause for concern to find about health problems that may affect your dog. But it is important to bear in mind that some basic knowledge is an asset, allowing you to spot signs of trouble at an early stage. Early diagnosis is very often the means to the most effective treatment.

Fortunately, the GSP is a generally healthy and disease-free dog with his only visits to the vet being annual check-ups. In most cases, owners can look forward to enjoying many happy years with this outstanding companion.

Useful addresses

Breed & Kennel Clubs

Please contact your Kennel Club to obtain contact information about breed clubs in your area.

UK

The Kennel Club (UK)
1 Clarges Street London, W1J 8AB
Telephone: 0870 606 6750
Fax: 0207 518 1058
Web: www.thekennelclub.org.uk

USA

American Kennel Club (AKC)
5580 Centerview Drive, Raleigh, NC 27606.
Telephone: 919 233 9767
Fax: 919 233 3627
Email: info@akc.org
Web: www.akc.org

United Kennel Club (UKC)
100 E Kilgore Rd, Kalamazoo,
MI 49002-5584, USA.
Tel: 269 343 9020
Fax: 269 343 7037
Web:www.ukcdogs.com/

Australia

Australian National Kennel Council (ANKC)
The Australian National Kennel Council is the administrative body for pure breed canine affairs in Australia. It does not, however, deal directly with dog exhibitors, breeders or judges. For information pertaining to breeders, clubs or shows, please contact the relevant State or Territory Body.

International

Fédération Cynologique Internationalé (FCI)
Place Albert 1er, 13, B-6530 Thuin, Belgium.
Tel: +32 71 59.12.38
Fax: +32 71 59.22.29
Web: www.fci.be/

Training and behavior

UK

Association of Pet Dog Trainers
Telephone: 01285 810811
Web: http://www.apdt.co.uk

Canine Behaviour
Association of Pet Behaviour Counsellors
Telephone: 01386 751151
Web: http://www.apbc.org.uk/

USA

Association of Pet Dog Trainers
Tel: 1 800 738 3647
Web: www.apdt.com/

American College of Veterinary Behaviorists
Web: http://dacvb.org/

American Veterinary Society of Animal Behavior
Web: www.avsabonline.org/

Australia

APDT Australia Inc
Web: www.apdt.com.au

For details of regional behaviorists, contact the relevant State or Territory Controlling Body.

Activities
UK
Agility Club
http://www.agilityclub.co.uk/

British Flyball Association
Telephone: 01628 829623
Web: http://www.flyball.org.uk/

USA
North American Dog Agility Council
Web: www.nadac.com/

North American Flyball Association, Inc.
Tel/Fax: 800 318 6312
Web: www.flyball.org/

Australia
Agility Dog Association of Australia
Tel: 0423 138 914
Web: www.adaa.com.au/

NADAC Australia
Web: www.nadacaustralia.com/

Australian Flyball Association
Tel: 0407 337 939
Web: www.flyball.org.au/

International
World Canine Freestyle Organisation
Tel: (718) 332-8336
Web: www.worldcaninefreestyle.org

Health
UK
British Small Animal Veterinary Association
Tel: 01452 726700
Web: http://www.bsava.com/

Royal College of Veterinary Surgeons
Tel: 0207 222 2001
Web: www.rcvs.org.uk

www.dogbooksonline.co.uk/healthcare/

Alternative Veterinary Medicine Centre
Tel: 01367 710324
Web: www.alternativevet.org/

USA
American Veterinary Medical Association
Tel: 800 248 2862
Web: www.avma.org

American College of Veterinary Surgeons
Tel: 301 916 0200
Toll Free: 877 217 2287
Web: www.acvs.org/

Canine Eye Registration Foundation
The Veterinary Medical DataBases
1717 Philo Rd, PO Box 3007,
Urbana, IL 61803-3007
Tel: 217-693-4800
Fax: 217-693-4801
Web: http://www.vmdb.org/cerf.html

Orthopaedic Foundation of Animals
2300 E Nifong Boulevard
Columbia, Missouri, 65201-3806
Tel: 573 442-0418
Fax: 573 875-5073
Web: http://www.offa.org/

American Holistic Veterinary Medical
Association
Tel: 410 569 0795
Web: www.ahvma.org/

Australia
Australian Small Animal Veterinary
Association
Tel: 02 9431 5090
Web: www.asava.com.au

Australian Veterinary Association
Tel: 02 9431 5000
Web: www.ava.com.au

Australian College Veterinary Scientists
Tel: 07 3423 2016
Web: http://acvsc.org.au

Australian Holistic Vets
Web: www.ahv.com.au/